Read All About Whales

TOOTHED WHALES

Jason Cooper

The Rourke Corporation, Inc.
Vero Beach, Florida 32964

PHOTO CREDITS
©Thomas Kitchin: p.4, 7, 15, 21; ©Mike Nolan/INNERSPACE VISIONS: p.12; ©Doug Perrine/INNERSPACE VISIONS: p.10, 18; ©Brandon Cole: p.22; ©Lynn M. Stone: cover, p.6, 16, 19; ©Marty Snyderman: p.9; ©1996 Sea World of Florida, All rights reserved: p.13

Library of Congress Cataloging-in-Publication Data

Cooper, Jason, 1942-
    Toothed whales / by Jason Cooper
        p. cm. — (Read all about whales)
    Includes index.
    Summary: Describes different kinds of toothed whales, including the sperm whale, beluga, and killer whale.
    ISBN 0-86593-448-7
    1. Toothed whales—Juvenile literature. [1. Toothed whales. 2. Whales.]
I. Title II. Series: Cooper, Jason, 1942- Read all about whales
QL737.C43C66 1996
599.5'3—dc20   96–19190
                                                         CIP
                                                          AC

Printed in the USA

TABLE OF CONTENTS

TOOTHED WHALES

Most kinds of whales, including porpoises and dolphins, have mouths full of teeth. These are the toothed whales. Some 66 of the world's **species** (SPEE sheez), or kinds, of whales are toothed.

The other 10 species of whales have **baleen** (buh LEEN) in their jaws instead of teeth. Baleen are tough, comblike plates that trap food from seawater.

Whales are very unusual **mammals** (MAM uhlz). Unlike people and most other mammals, whales spend their entire lives in water.

The killer whale, or orca, is one of more than 65 species of whales with teeth.

KINDS OF TOOTHED WHALES

The species of toothed whales differ somewhat in size, shape, and habits. They also differ in the number, size, and shape of teeth. Scientists place toothed whales in several groups, such as the porpoises.

Toothed whales like these dolphins usually travel in groups called pods.

A family of killer whales chases a school of salmon in British Columbia, Canada.

Toothed whales are somewhat alike also. Most of them eat fish and squid, and they travel in **pods** (PAHDS), or groups.

Sometimes members of a pod help each other to hunt by herding fish into a tight school. Then the whales attack more easily.

FINDING PREY

Toothed whales can find prey, and each other, with **echolocation** (EK o lo KAY shun). When a whale sends out a sound underwater, the sound wave strikes an object. The echo of that sound returns to the whale. A whale can "read" the echo.

The whale can tell where something is and where it's going. It can also tell how big an object is and whether it's good to eat!

Many scientists believe that some toothed whales send out sound waves powerful enough to injure their prey.

Toothed whales use echolocation to find objects underwater.

SPERM WHALES

The sperm whale is a giant among toothed whales. It can grow 60 feet long and weigh 200,000 pounds. A close cousin, the pygmy sperm whale, reaches just 12 feet in length.

The sperm whale has a huge, blocky head. Its lower jaw, though, is long and slender with 16 to 30 peg-shaped teeth.

It is a remarkable diver. It can plunge over a mile deep into the sea and can stay underwater for more than an hour.

The great sperm whale is the largest of the toothed whales.

DOLPHINS AND PORPOISES

Common names in the whale family are confusing. "Whale" generally refers to the biggest members of the group. But some whales are fairly small. Sometimes porpoises are called dolphins and dolphins are called porpoises.

Dolphins and porpoises move swiftly through the sea with their leaps.

Killer whales are the largest of the dolphins.

True porpoises are quite small, just 4 to 6 feet long. Porpoises have spade-shaped teeth.

Dolphins are 7 to 30 feet long. Dolphin teeth are cone-shaped.

The pilot whale and killer whale are both big dolphins.

BELUGAS AND NARWHALS

Belugas and narwhals are small whales of the icy cold Arctic seas. They look much different from other toothed whales.

Belugas are white when full grown. They're often called white whales.

Narwhals are even more unusual looking. Male narwhals have a strange, spearlike tusk. It is probably used in fights between the males.

The tusk is the narwhal's overgrown left tooth. It may be up to nine feet long and weigh more than 20 pounds.

The bullet-shaped beluga is the "white whale" of the Arctic seas.

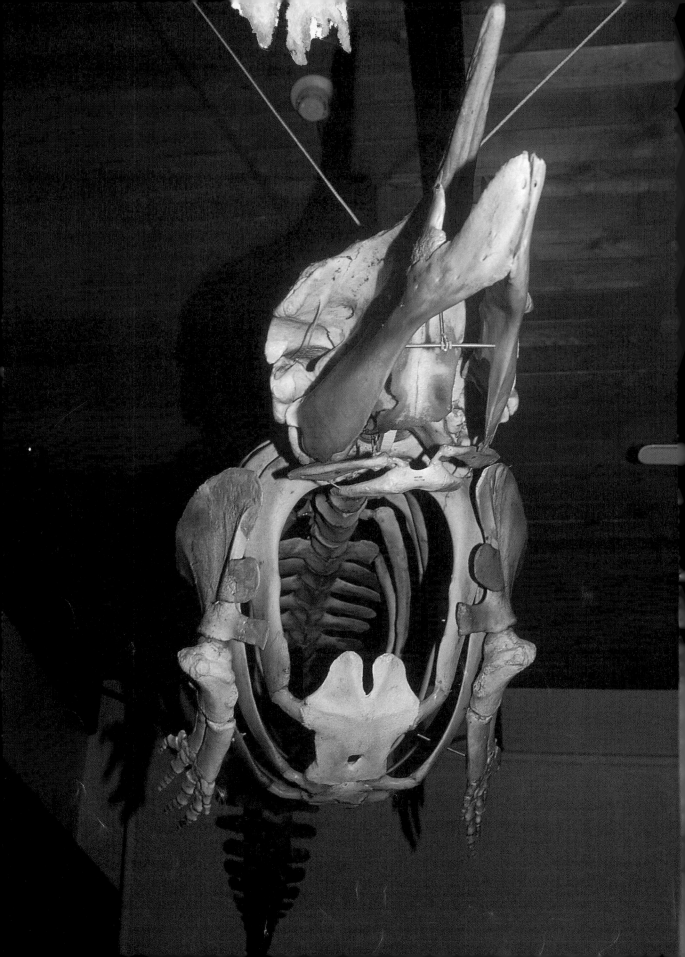

BEAKED WHALES

Beaked whales live in all the oceans, but nowhere do these whales have beaks. They do have a sharp, beaklike snout, however.

The 18 species of beaked whales have no upper teeth. They have just two to four teeth in their lower jaws.

Like most toothed whales, beaked whales live on fish and squid.

The biggest of the beaked whales reaches 40 feet in length. The smallest is just 15 feet.

Skeleton of a Bering Sea beaked whale shows the long snout of the species and the "hand" bones that are covered by whale's flippers.

BOTTLE-NOSED DOLPHIN

The bottle-nosed dolphin—often called porpoise—is the most widely known member of the whale family. They have been stars in movies, books, and TV shows.

Bottle-nosed dolphins are displayed in many zoos and **aquariums** (uh KWAR ee uhmz). They can be trained to perform on command.

Leaping ability of the bottle-nosed dolphin makes it a favorite in sea animal shows.

Bottle-nosed dolphins have lightning speed in the water. Speed and teeth help them keep their bellies full of fish.

Pods of bottle-nosed dolphins are often seen swimming along the coasts of Florida. Their up-and-down style of swimming is called "porpoising."

These dolphins have been widely studied. Their large brains seem to be most useful in their echolocation skills.

KILLER WHALES

Killer whales, also known as orcas, can grow to be 30 feet long and weigh 20,000 pounds. The sleek black-and-white orcas are the largest of the dolphins.

Some pods of orcas feed on seals and sea lions. Others seem to be strictly fish eaters.

These animals earned the name "Killer" because they were the only whales known to feed on other mammals.

Sunset strikes the tall dorsal, or back, fin of a killer whale along the British Columbia coast.

GLOSSARY

aquarium (uh KWAR ee uhm) — a container, such as a glass tank, for keeping fish and other animals of the water; a public place where animals of the water are shown

baleen (buh LEEN) — the tough, comblike plates found in the upper jaws of certain whales; whalebone

echolocation (EK o lo KAY shun)   a whale's system of using echoes to locate food and its surroundings underwater

mammals (MAM uhlz) — the group of air-breathing, warm-blooded, milk-producing animals

pod (PAHD) — a group of whales, porpoises, or dolphins

species (SPEE sheez) — within a group of closely related animals, one certain kind, such as a *bottle-nosed* dolphin

With power, speed, and gracefulness, a wild killer whale leaps from the sea. The reason for a whale's leaps is a mystery to scientists.

23

INDEX